Jazz Hanon
PLAY-ALONG

By Peter Deneff

Speed • Pitch • Balance • Loop

To access audio visit:
www.halleonard.com/mylibrary
Enter Code
4855-3014-2245-2975

ISBN 978-1-61780-722-0

HAL•LEONARD®

Copyright © 2001 by HAL LEONARD CORPORATION
International Copyright Secured All Rights Reserved

No part of this publication may be reproduced in any form or by
any means without the prior written permission of the Publisher.

Visit Hal Leonard Online at
www.halleonard.com

Contact us:
Hal Leonard
7777 West Bluemound Road
Milwaukee, WI 53213
Email: info@halleonard.com

In Europe, contact:
Hal Leonard Europe Limited
42 Wigmore Street
Marylebone, London, W1U 2RN
Email: info@halleonardeurope.com

In Australia, contact:
Hal Leonard Australia Pty. Ltd.
4 Lentara Court
Cheltenham, Victoria, 3192 Australia
Email: info@halleonard.com.au

This book is dedicated to
George V. Deneff

About the author

Peter Deneff grew up in Long Beach, California listening to Greek and classical music and studying classical piano with Leaine Gibson. After starting his professional life playing in a Greek wedding band at age fifteen, he became obsessed with straight-ahead and Latin jazz. He began jazz studies with renowned pianist Mike Garson, where he crafted his art through studying some of the great jazz improvisers such as Charlie Parker, Bud Powell, and Chick Corea. During this time he also studied many ethnic styles that eventually led to the development of his classical and jazz compositional style as well as the formation of his Middle Eastern-Latin jazz group *Excursion (www.excursionjazz.com)*. He also pursued undergraduate and graduate studies in classical composition and film scoring at California State University Long Beach under the direction of Dr. Justus Matthews, Dr. Martin Herman and Perry Lamarca. Peter has written several best-selling books for Hal Leonard Publishing including *Jazz Hanon, Blues Hanon,* and *Samba Hanon*. He has also composed and performed music for the Charles Sheen film, *Five Aces*. Deneff has performed at such varied venues as the Greek Theater, the Carpenter Performing Arts Center, the Playboy Jazz Festival, the Los Angeles Street Scene, the Orange County Street Fair, Universal Studios, the NAMM show, and the Baked Potato. His stylistic versatility has allowed him to play and/or sing with a diverse assortment of groups like Tierra, Ike Willis (singer with Frank Zappa), the Leslie Paula/Universal Studios Salsa Band, and Ebi, a notable Persian singer. Deneff also continues to play and record modern and folk Greek music for numerous events *(www.synthesimusic.com)* as well as an occasional Middle Eastern or jazz gig. Besides performing, Peter has also taught in many institutions such as Musician's Institute, Orange County High School of the Arts, and Cypress College, where he continues to teach classical and jazz piano. He spends most of his time in his studio producing projects for Yamaha Corporation *(Disklavier, Clavinova, Internet Direct Content)* and Hal Leonard Corporation *(Piano Play-Alongs, Instrumental Play-Alongs)*.

Introduction

Of all the different genres of music, I would consider jazz to be one of the most technically challenging, both mentally and physically. For instance, one must interpret the harmony of a jazz piece through a series of voicings. Furthermore, the jazz pianist is often expected to simultaneously craft an improvisation. As if this weren't enough of a challenge, they might also be required to give cues to the rest of the band. Blazing tempi, complex melodic lines and intricate harmonic progressions challenge even the most seasoned musicians.

With all of the cerebral resistance one deals with when navigating through a jazz tune, it would seem logical that the pianist should at least prepare their fingers for the task. I have always believed that a good musician should never be limited by their lack of good technique. Technique is not an end in itself but rather a "tool" in the pianist's "toolbox". Classical pianists by the nature of their repertoire seem to be exposed to technical exercises from an early age. Rarely have I come across a serious piano student who has not played through C.L. Hanon's *The Virtuoso Pianist*, Czerny or other books of finger exercises. It would seem impossible to venture through a Bach fugue or a Scriabin etude without proper technical preparation.

While the traditional books of piano technique are paramount in the study of most piano literature, they do not address many of the challenges the jazz pianist faces. Angular lines, large intervallic leaps, pentatonic patterns, irregular chromatic melodies, and unconventional (in a classical sense) fingerings need to be practiced in a formal and organized manner in order to be executed articulately and evenly. These are the things on which I concentrate most in this book. While traditional books of technique should not be discarded, these exercises will provide an invaluable source of challenging practice material for all pianists, but especially for those who play jazz. The beginner as well as the professional will find them useful for building, improving, and maintaining their physical ability.

There are many ways one could practice the studies in this book. In addition to being played as written and with the included background tracks, they can be played using a swing feel. Alternatively, the right hand lines can be played in unison with the left hand, "à la Oscar Peterson." Lastly, one can play the right hand part with the left and vise versa.

I did not include tempo markings because I don't believe in limiting how fast these exercises should be practiced. At the same time, however, they should never be played faster than they can be performed cleanly and free of mistakes. The key to playing fast is practicing slowly, and building the tempo incrementally. This is a practice technique that is almost always neglected by overzealous students! Some other techniques I like to use when practicing these exercises include the following:

- Start very slowly, deliberately, and staccato. This helps build articulation.
- Use a metronome. It will help build your sense of time.
- When you master an exercise at a given speed, increase the tempo **one notch** on your metronome.
- Keep your hands low profile and your fingers curved.
- Don't tense up. Monitor the tension in your **entire body**.
- Push yourself, but stop if you are experiencing pain. Technique exercises won't help you if you injure yourself!

Included in this edition are background tracks which are intended to enhance your practicing experience. The tempo of the audio tracks can be adjusted with the **PLAYBACK+** software. Of course, to fully benefit from the exercises, it is important to count carefully and practice at a reasonable tempo.

The main thing to keep in mind is that you should have fun with these exercises. Be creative and find new ways to incorporate these techniques into your music, jazz or otherwise. Last but not least, don't get discouraged by delayed progress. We all learn and develop at our own rate. Technique doesn't happen overnight. It may take weeks or even months to master some of these exercises, but when you do, you will have gained much of what is needed to become the next great jazz pianist!

Happy playing,
Peter Deneff

1

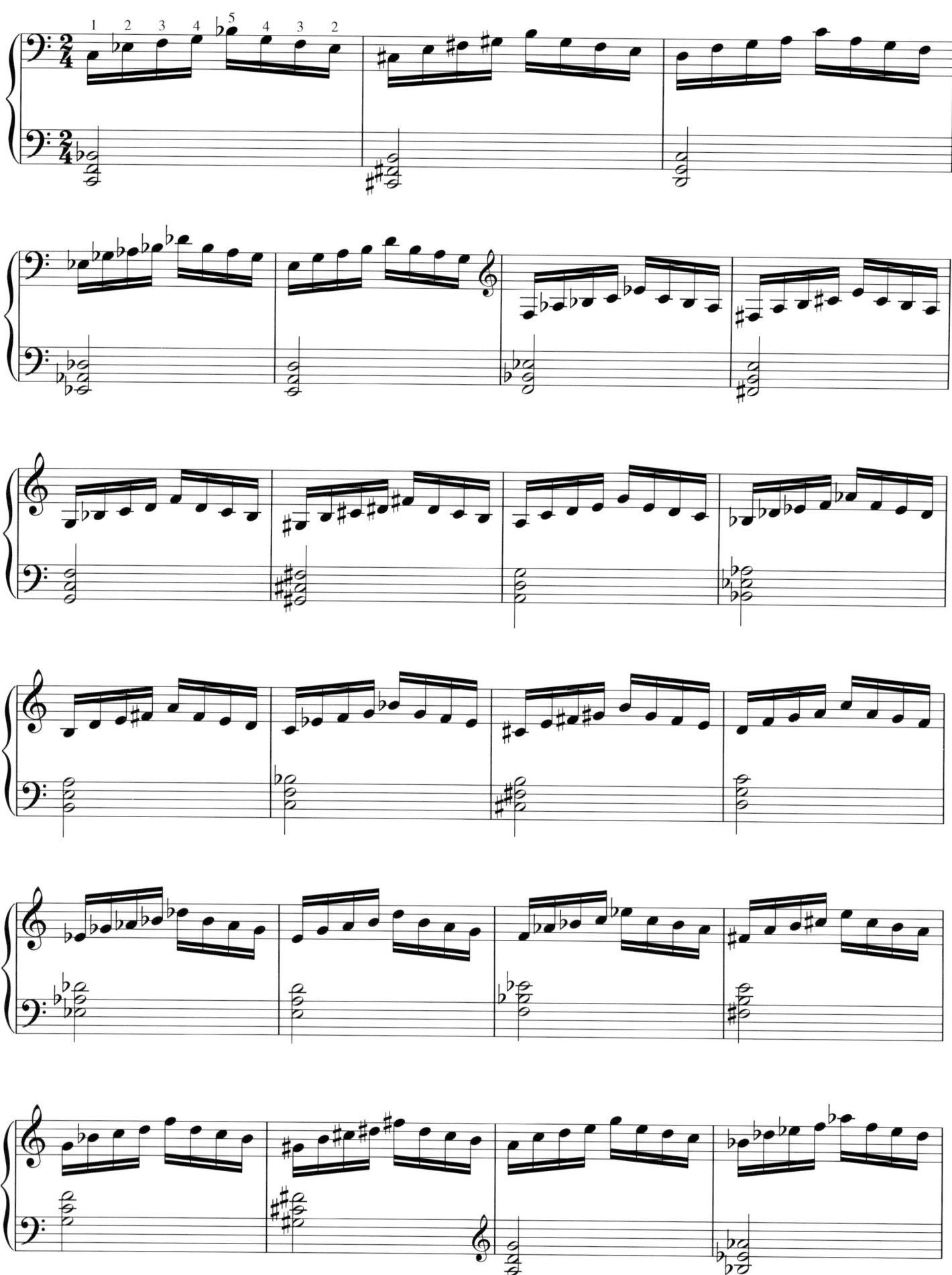

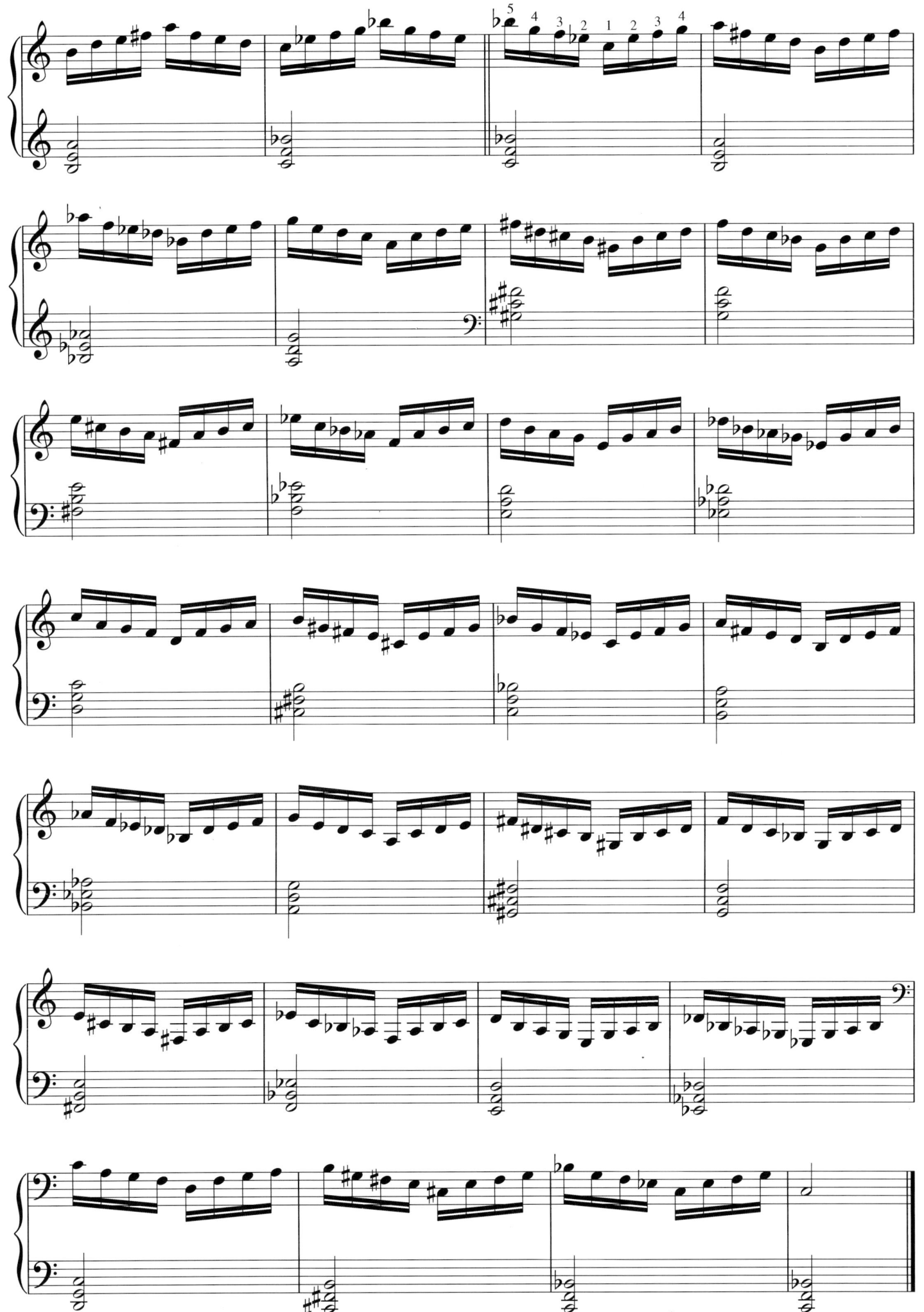

2

7

10

11

12

14

15

16

17

18

19

20

21

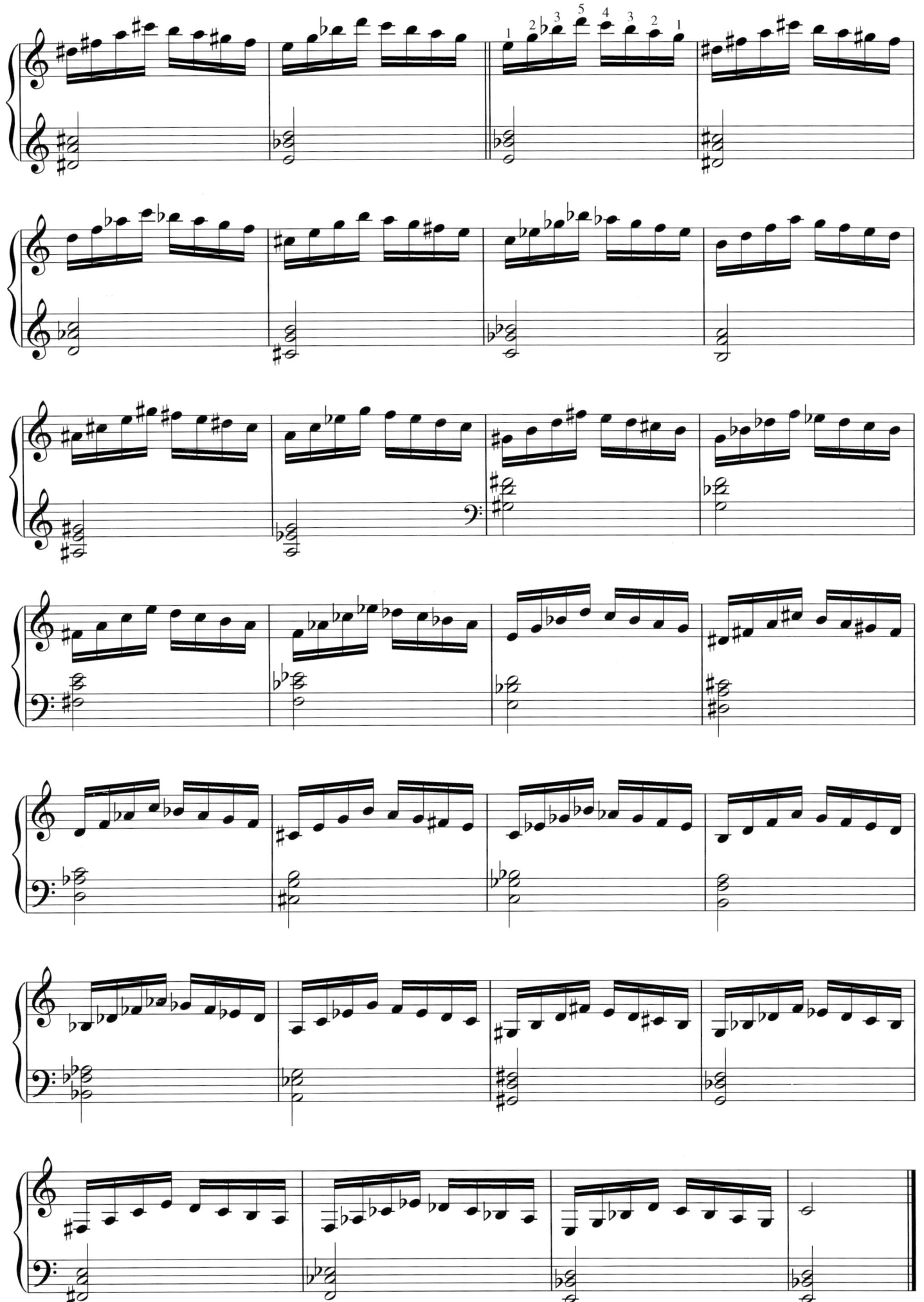

22

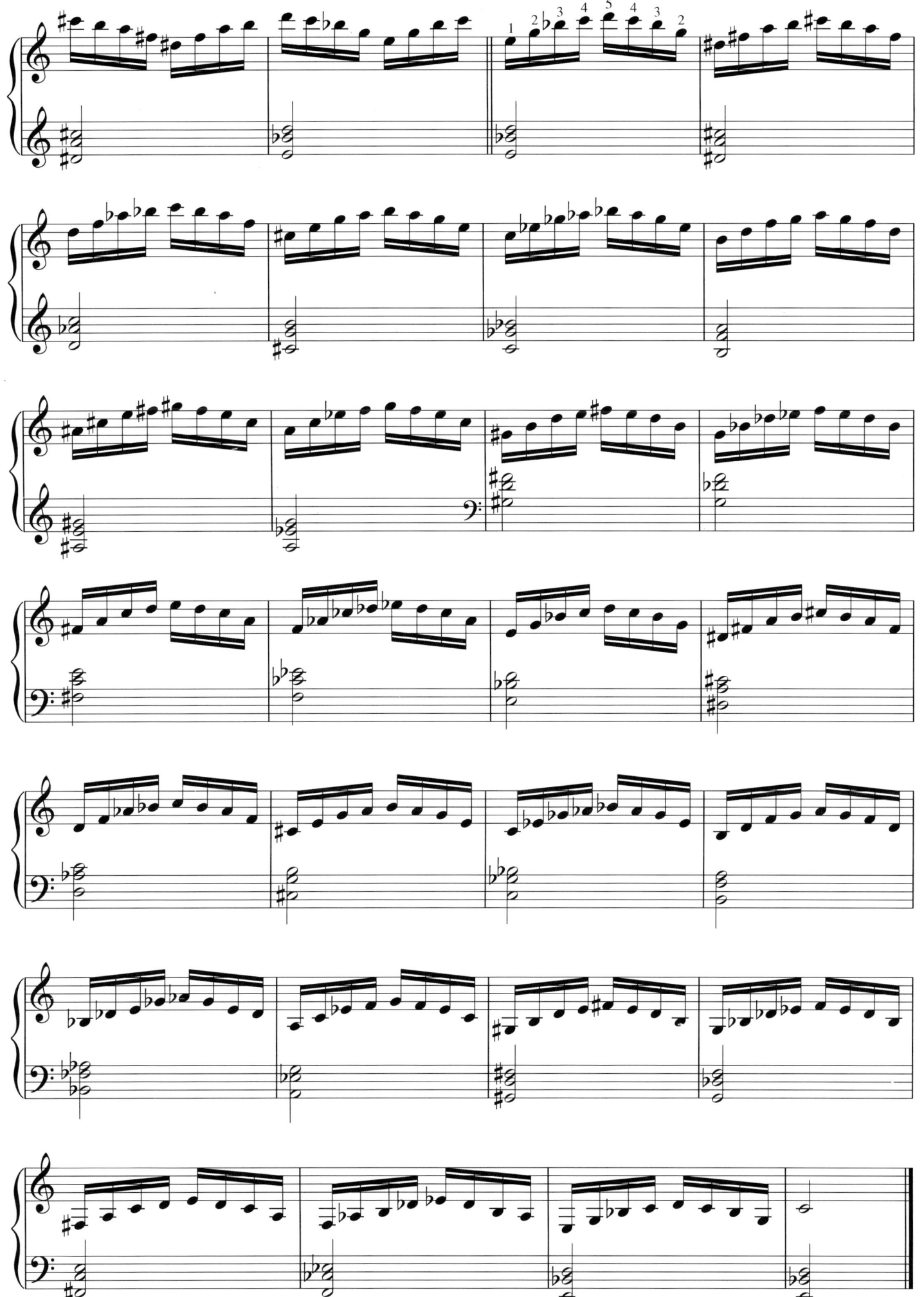

23

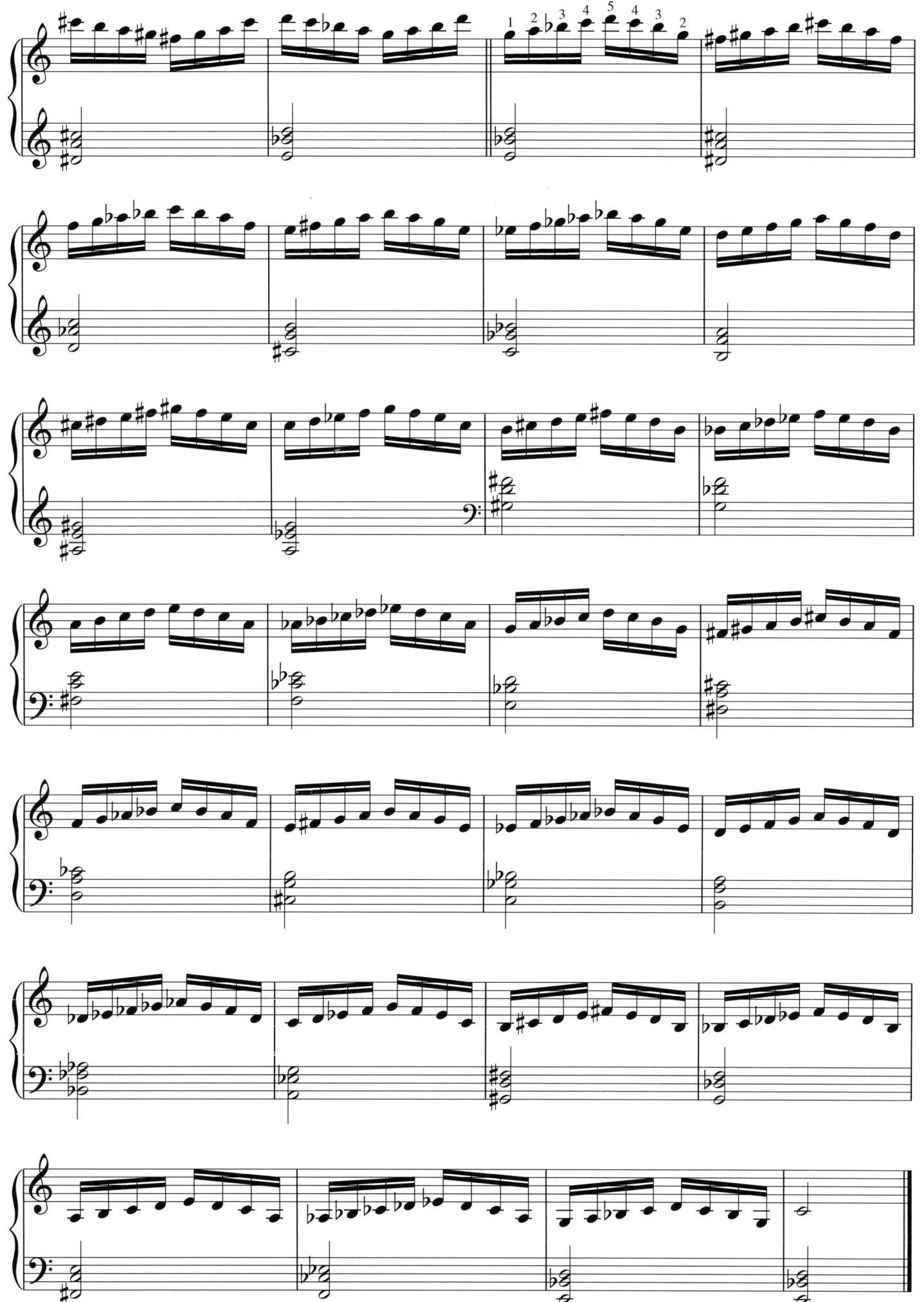

25

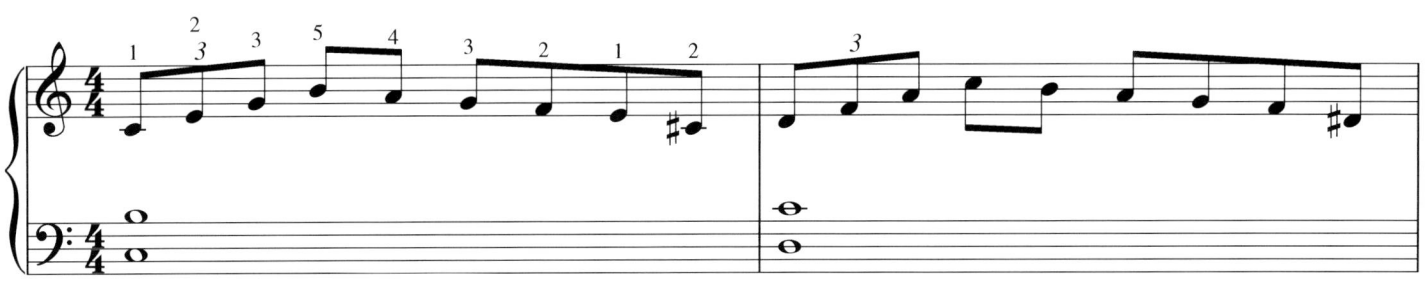

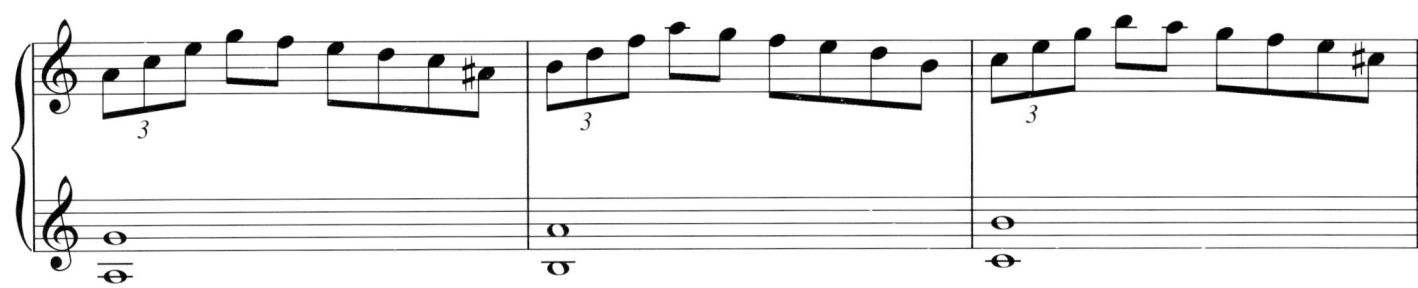
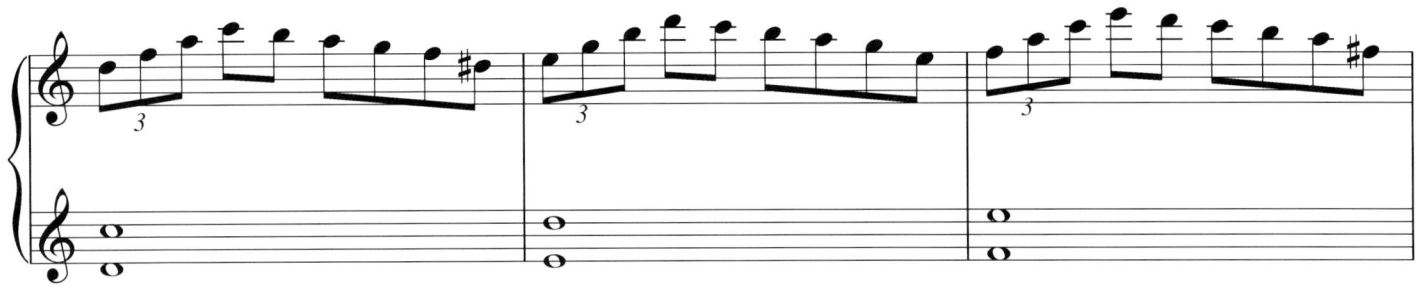

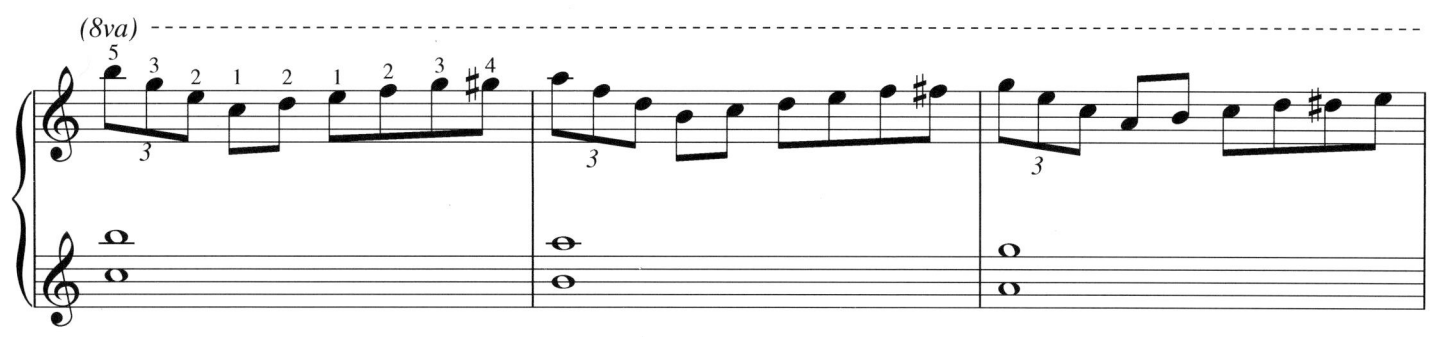

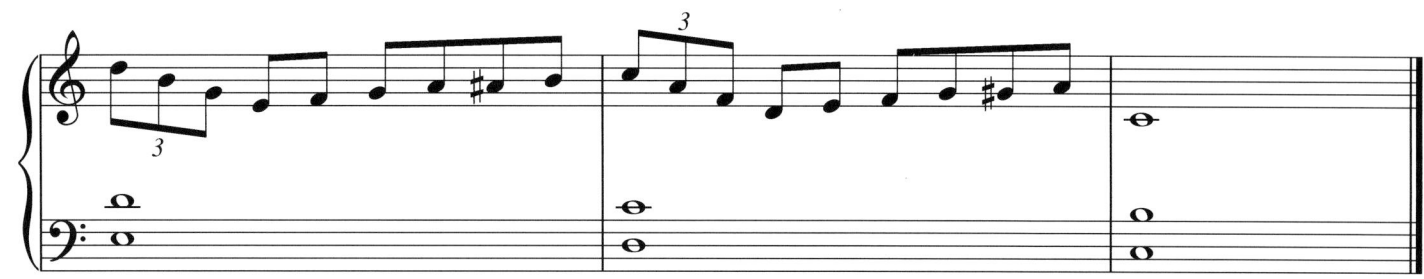

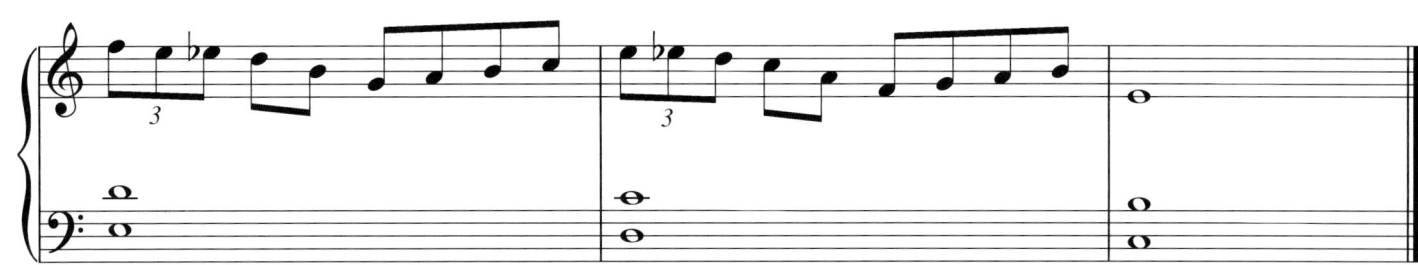

27

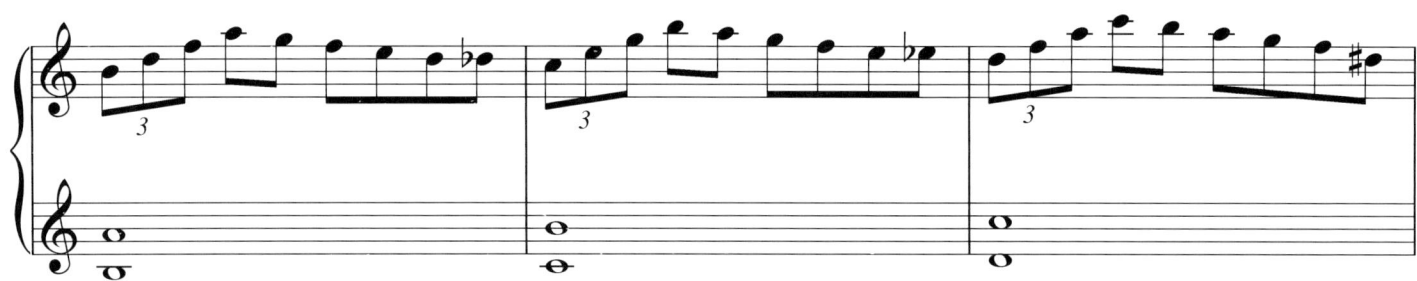
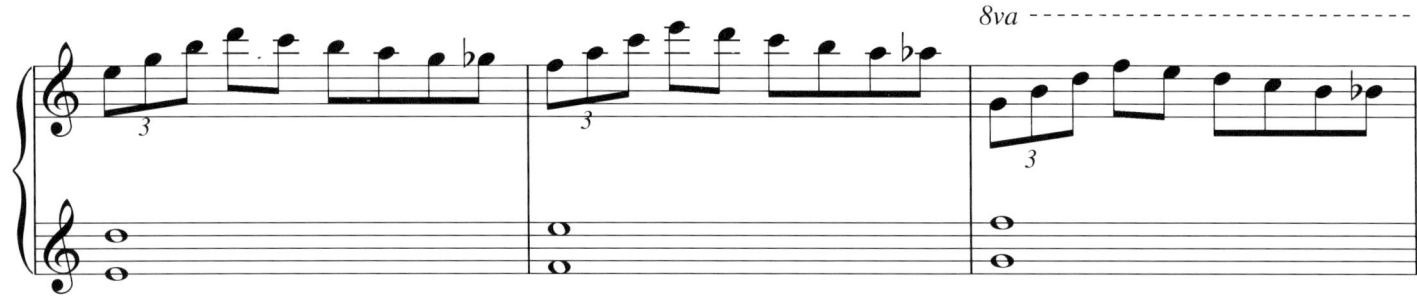

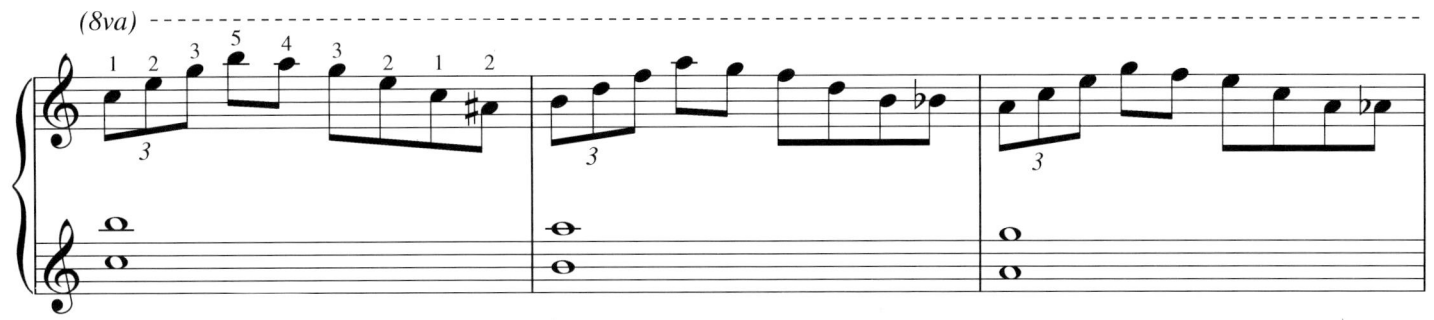
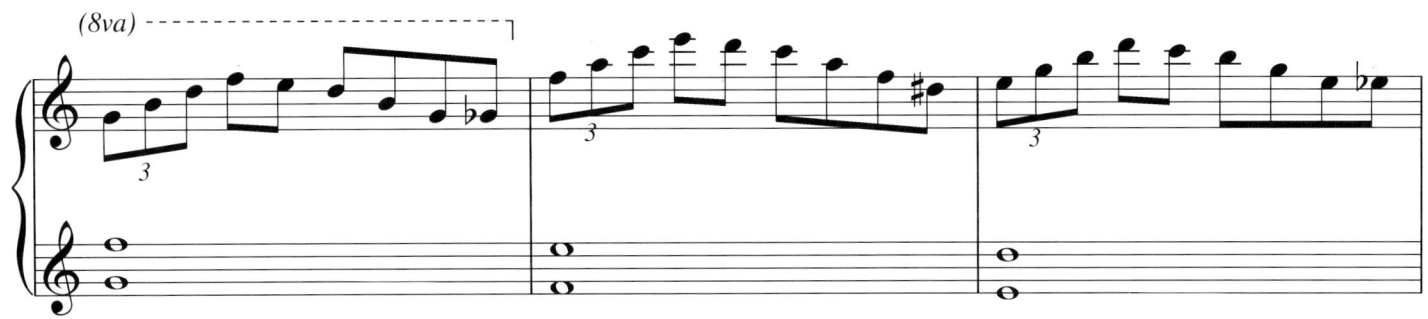
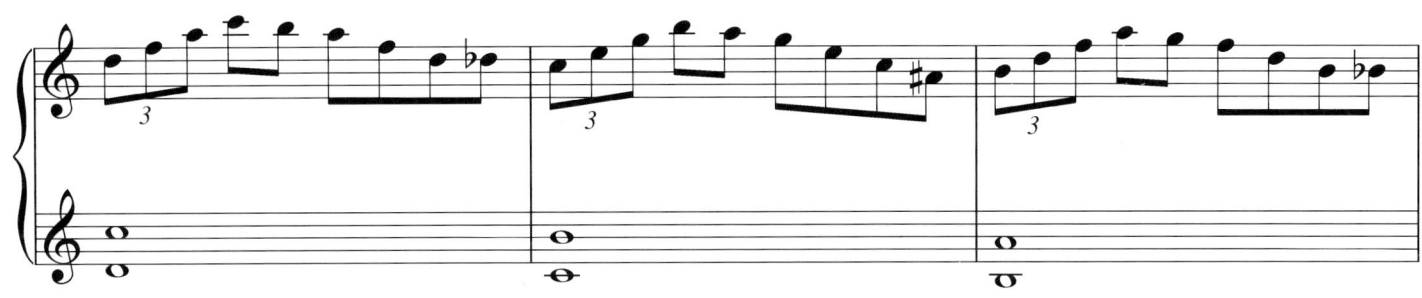

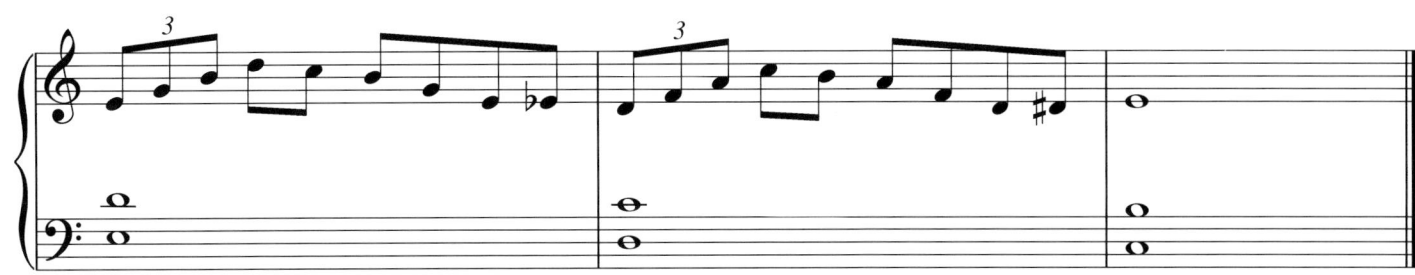

28

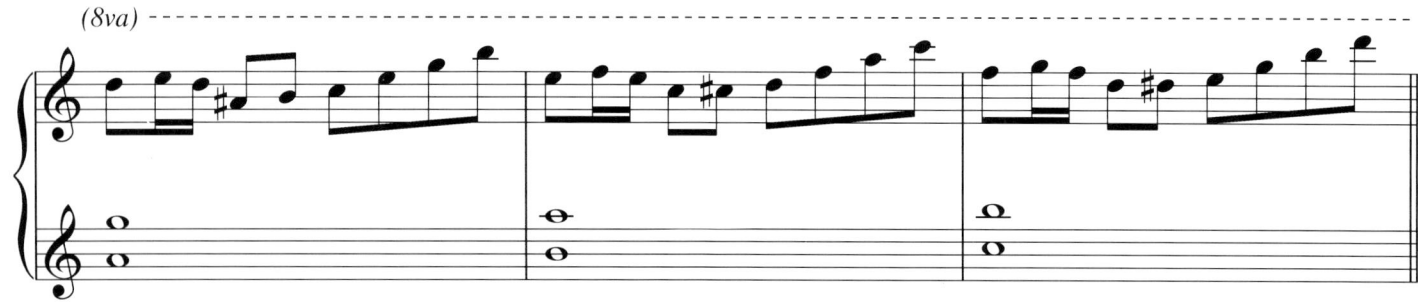

29

31

33

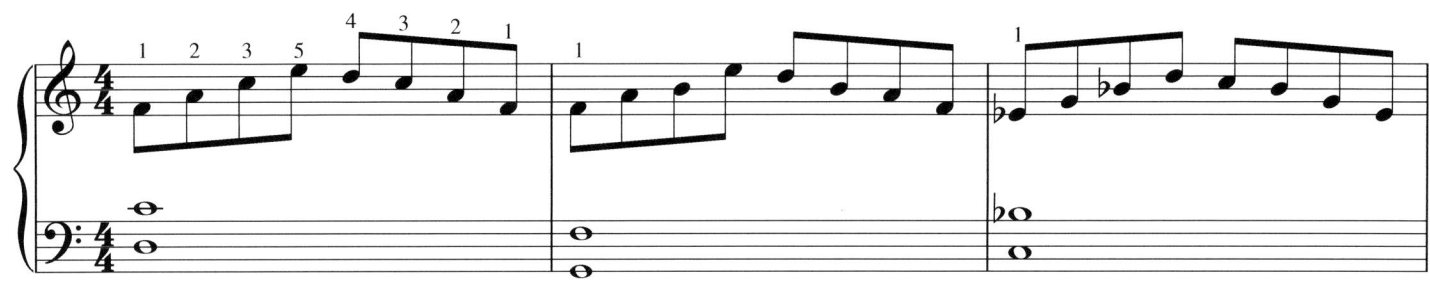
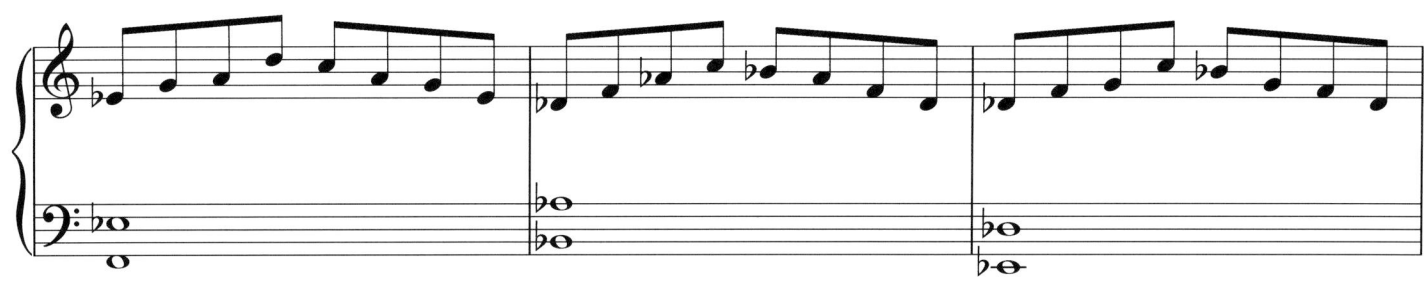
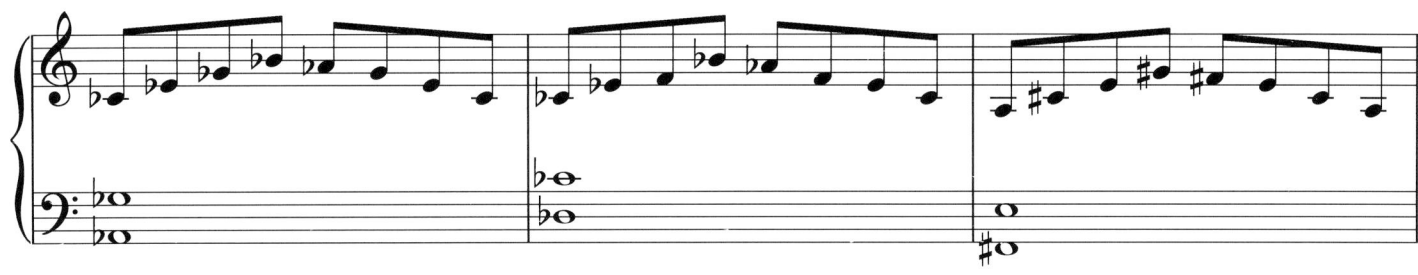

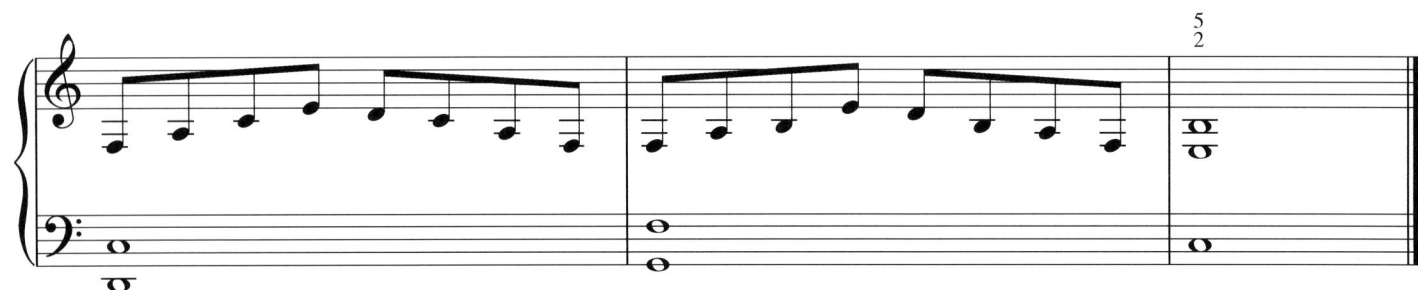

36

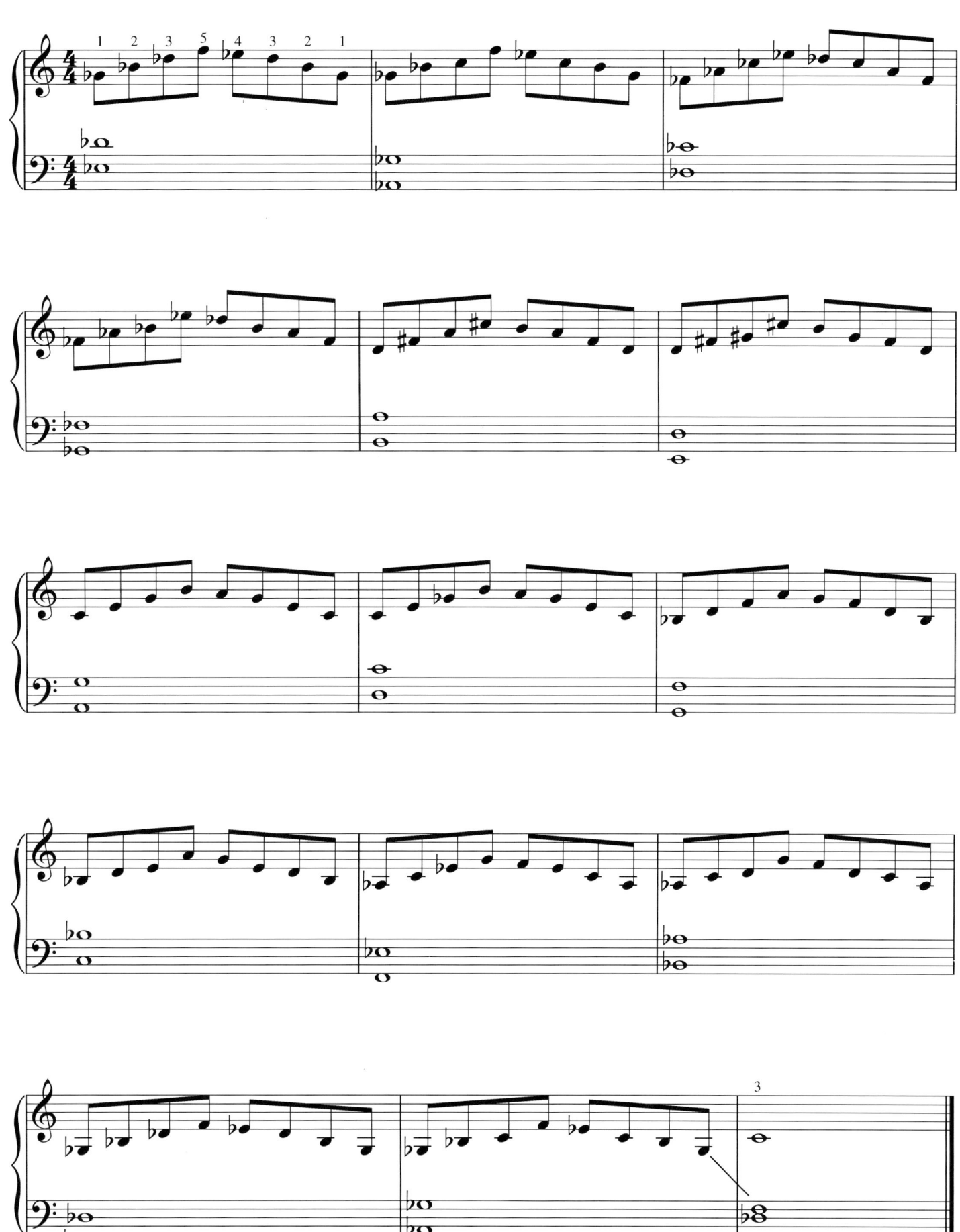

37

🔊 **39**

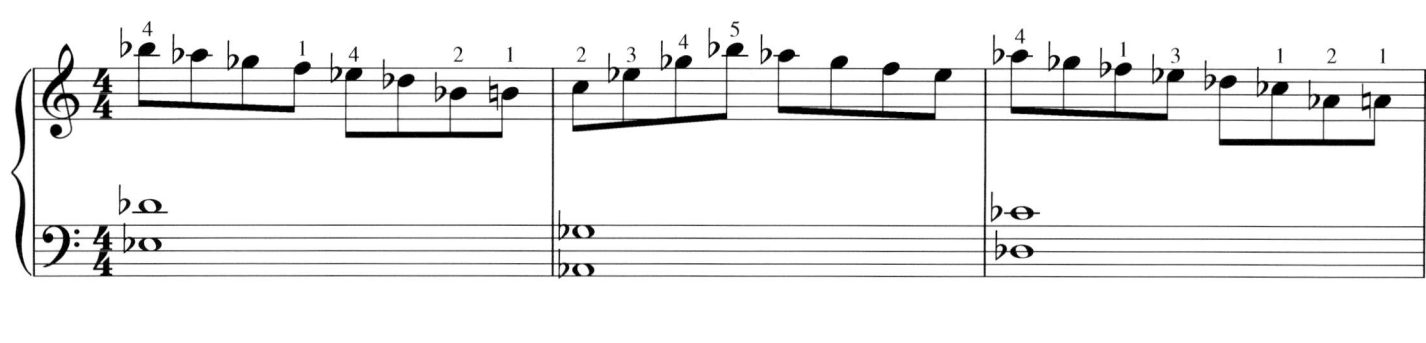

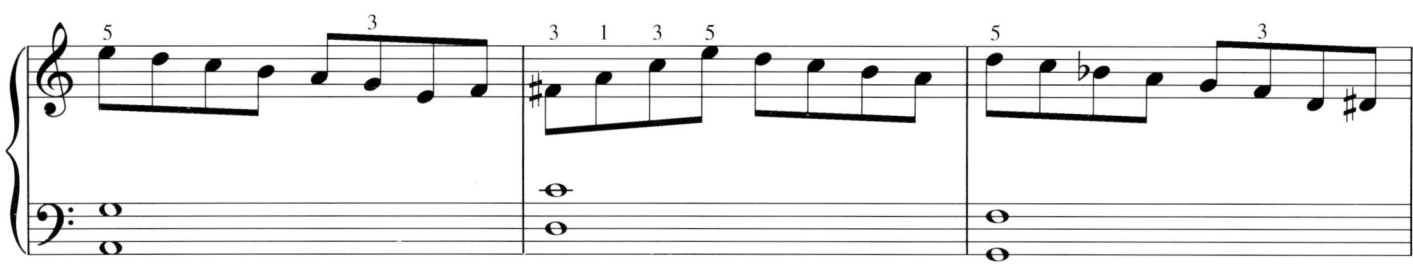

40

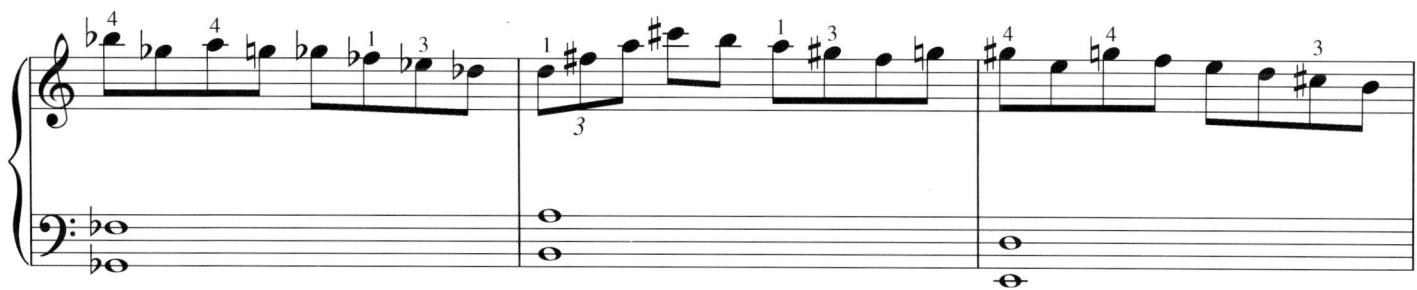
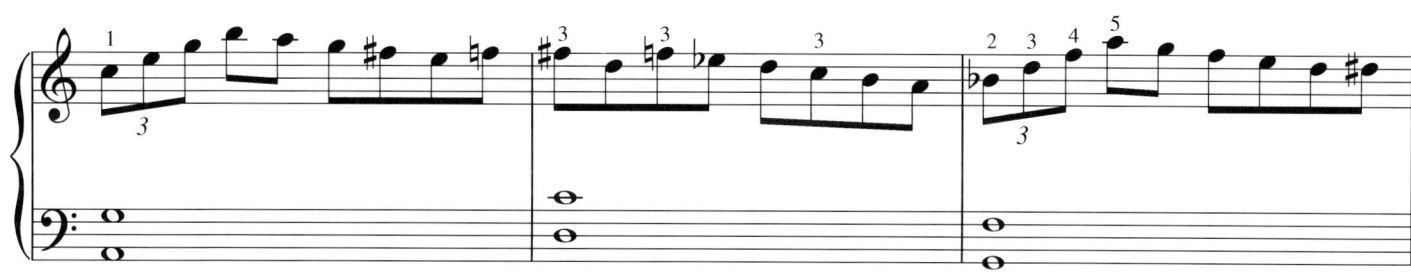
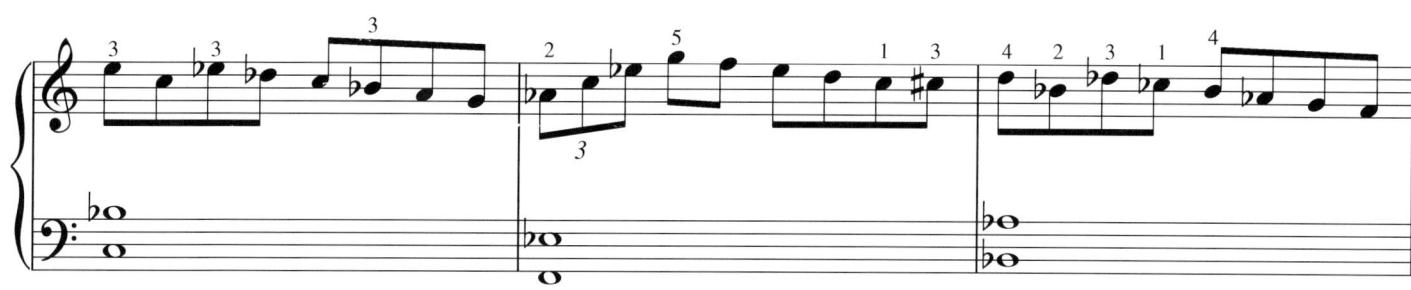

41

47

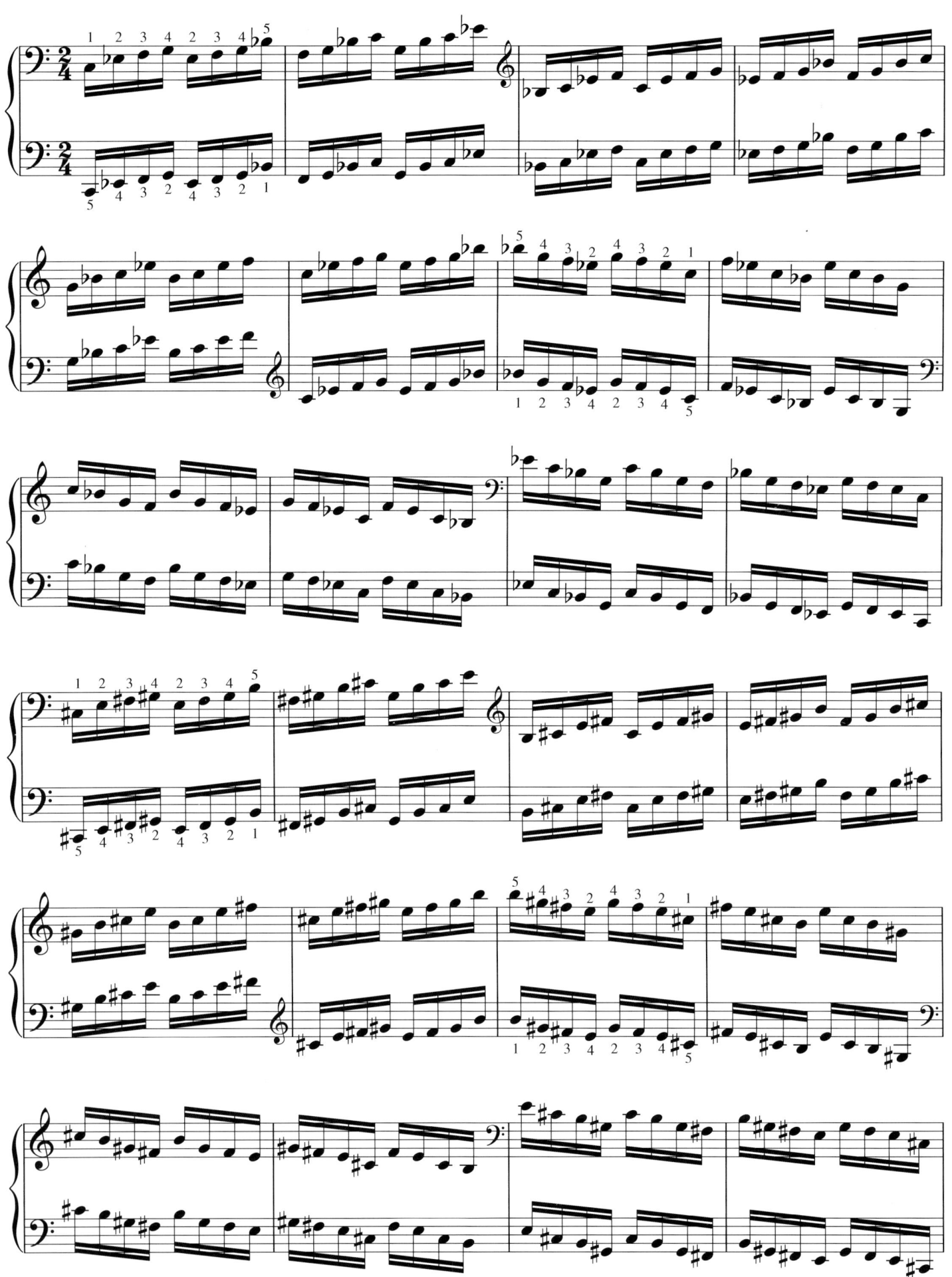

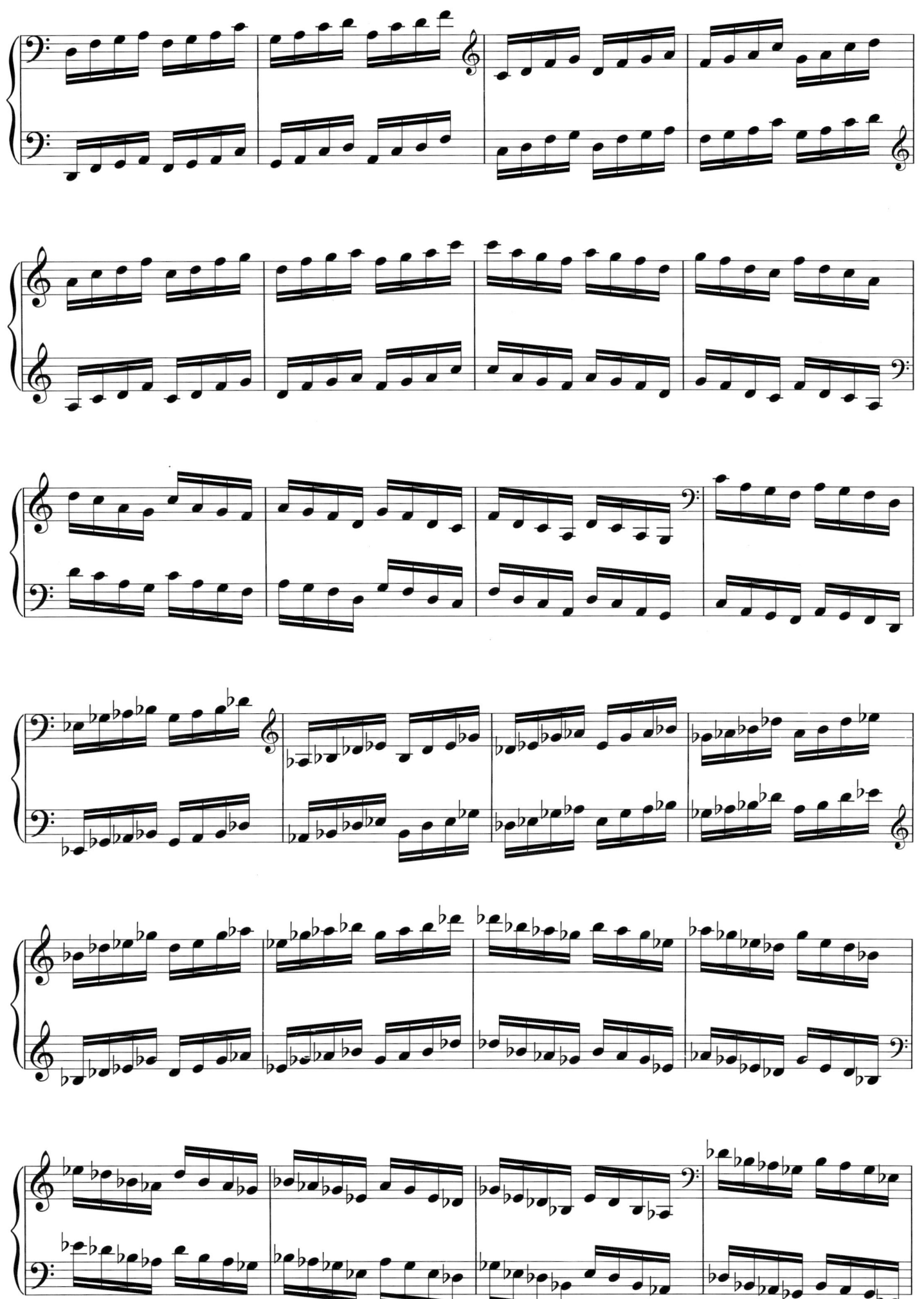

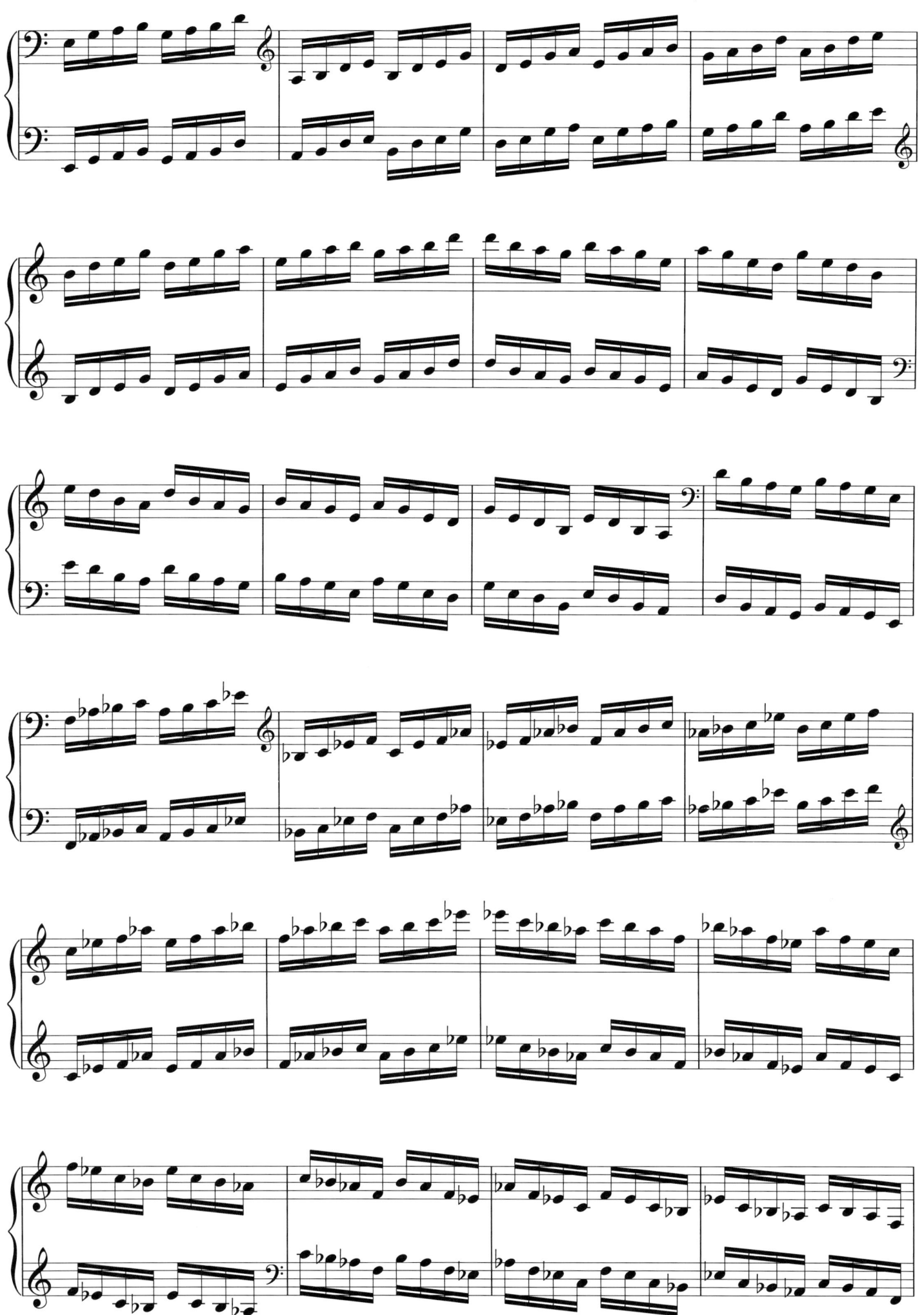

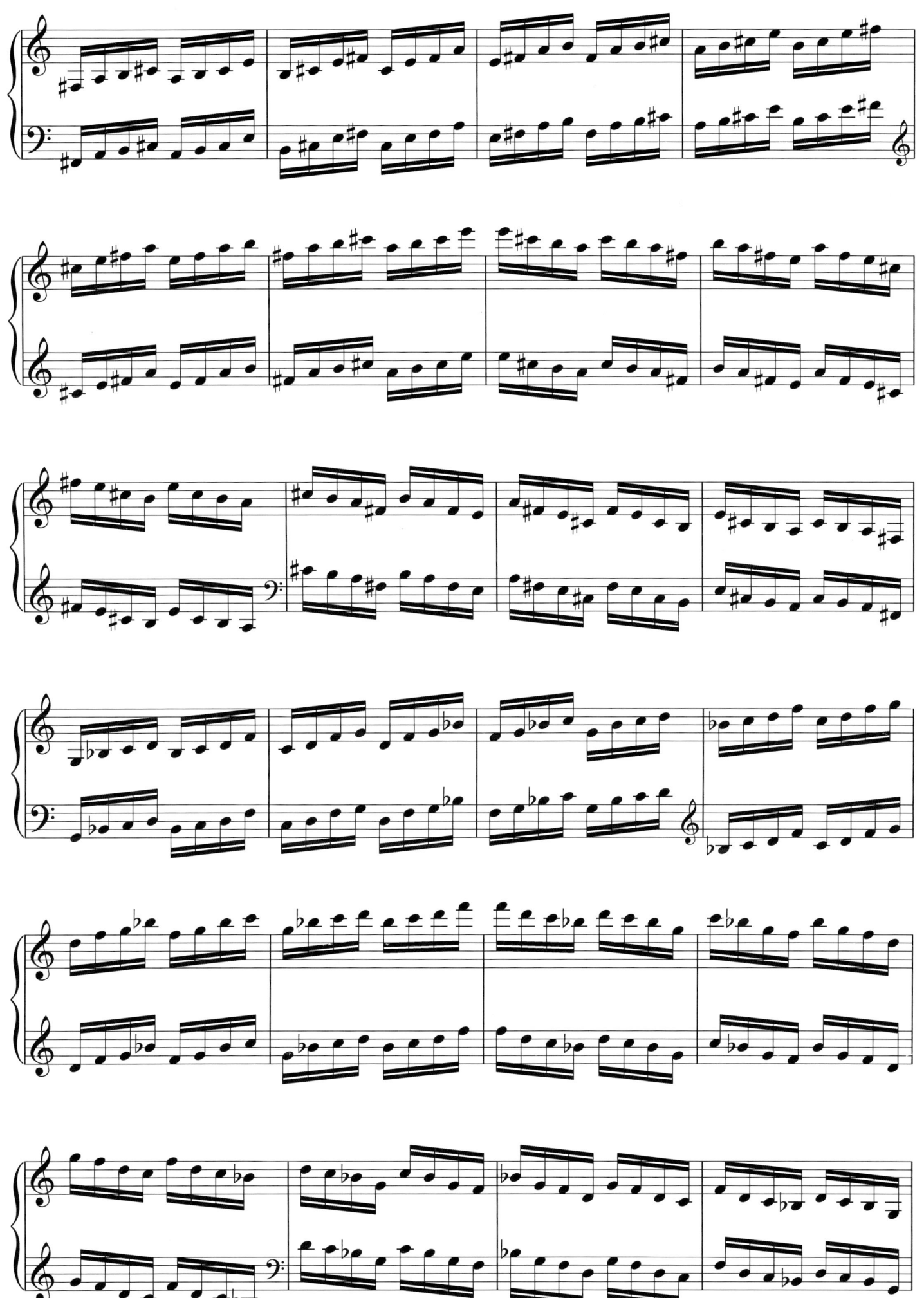

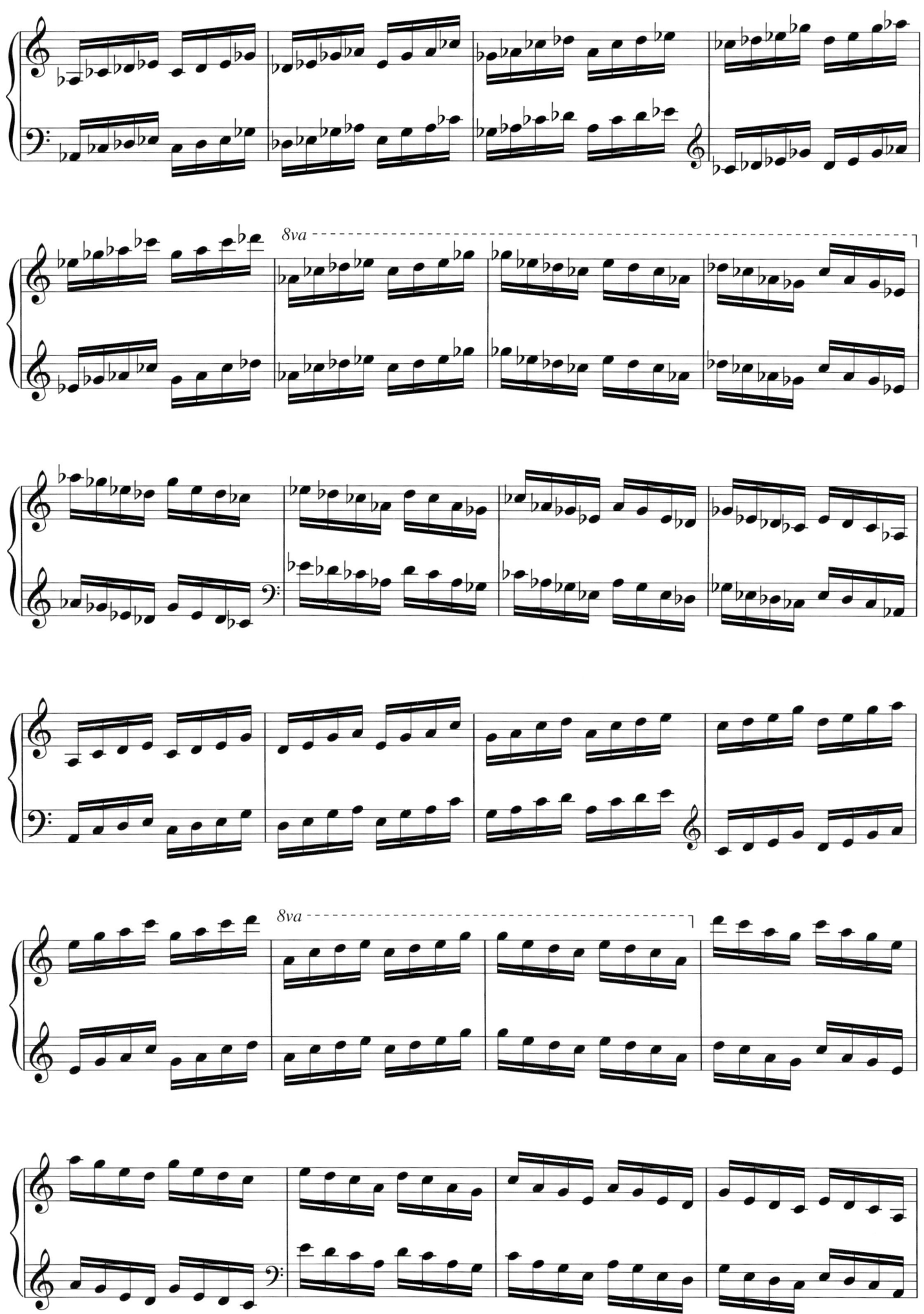

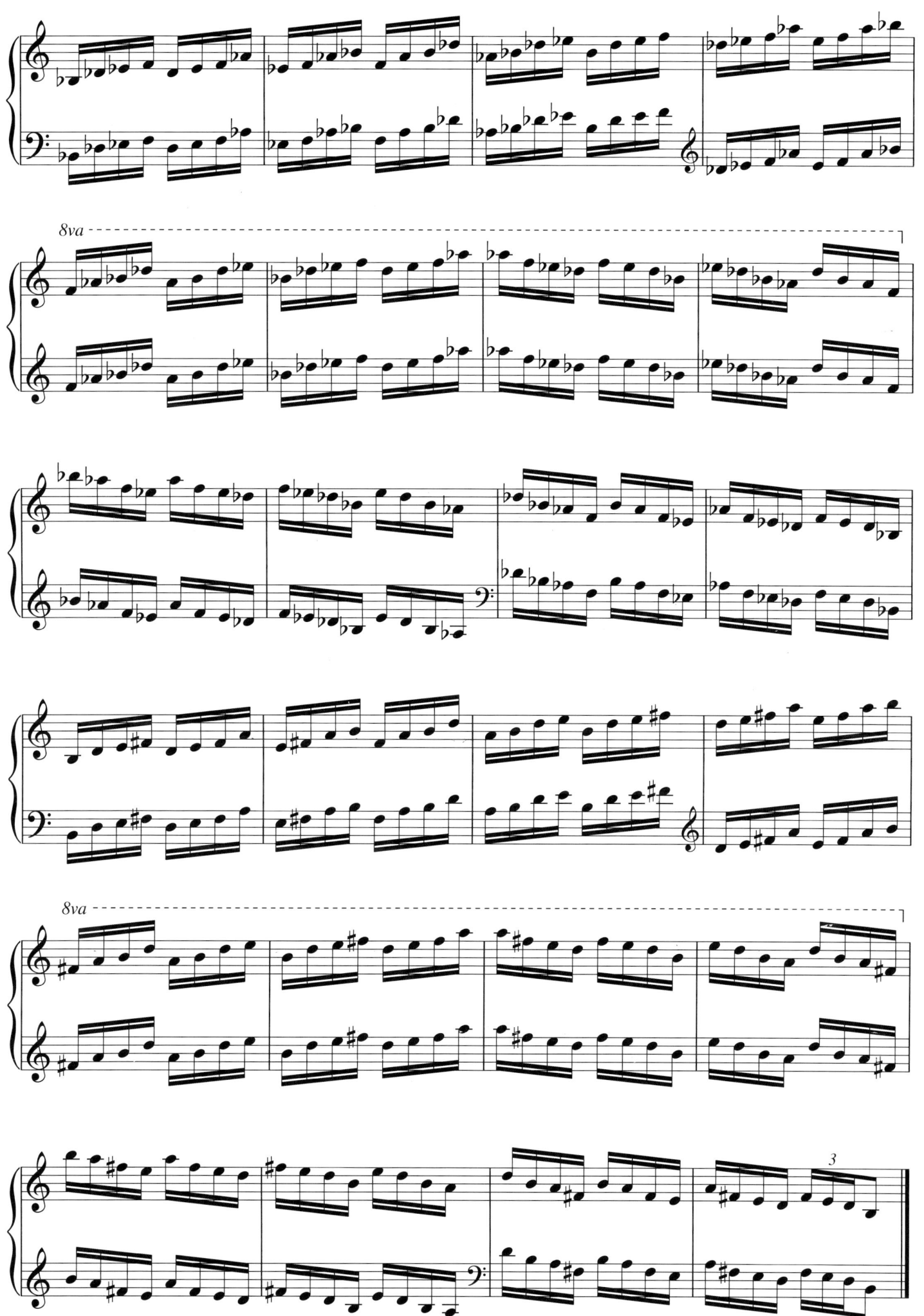

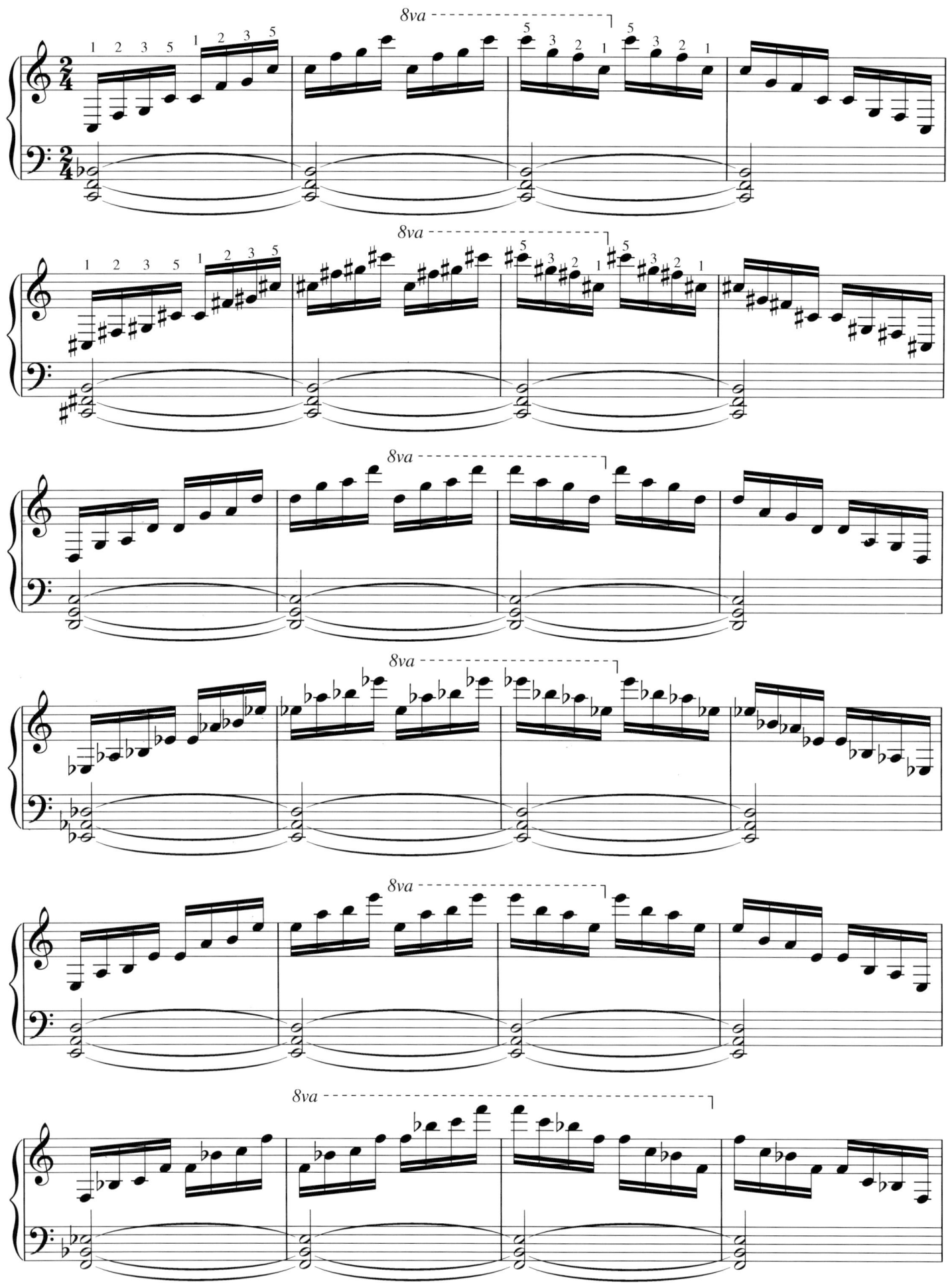

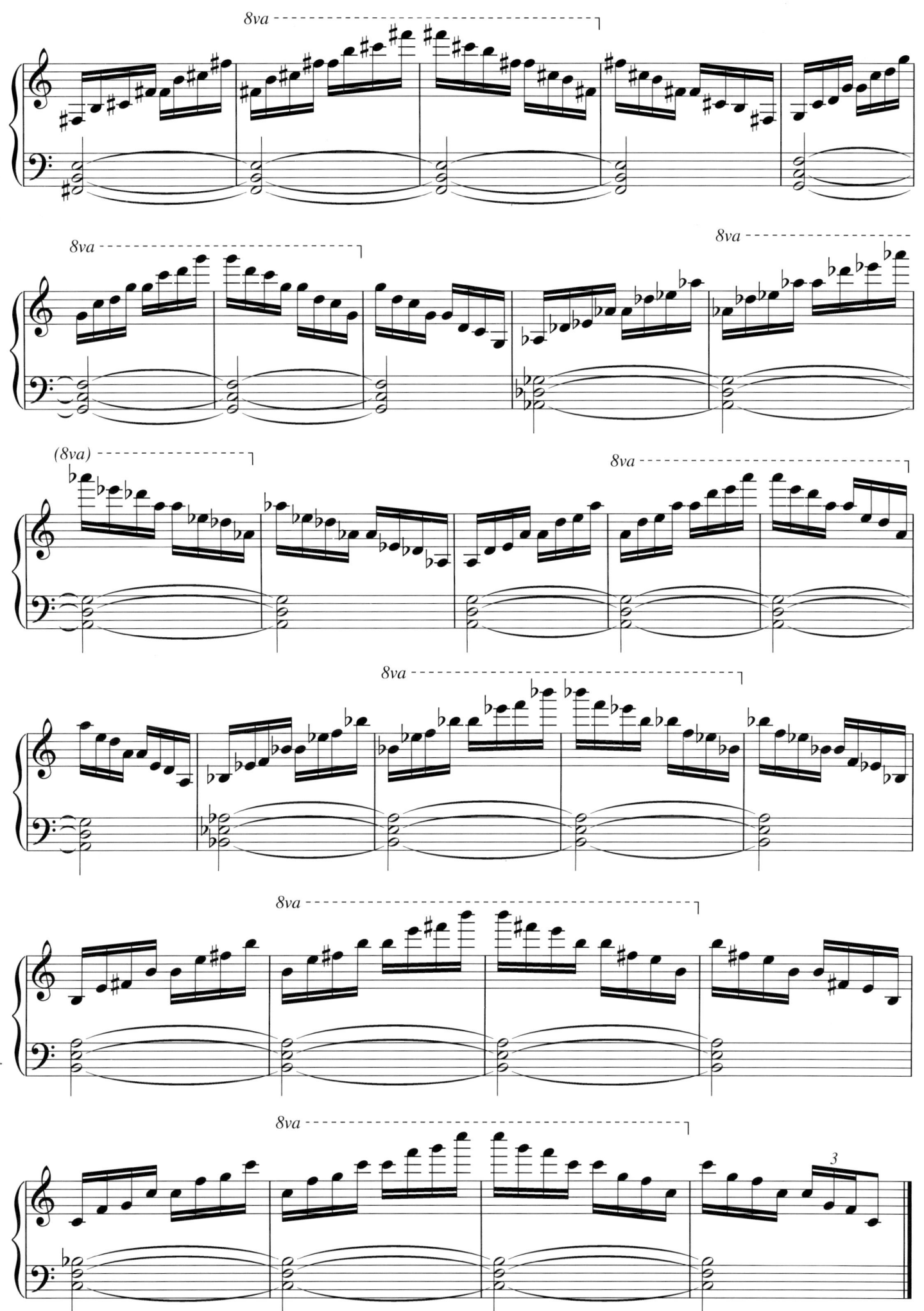

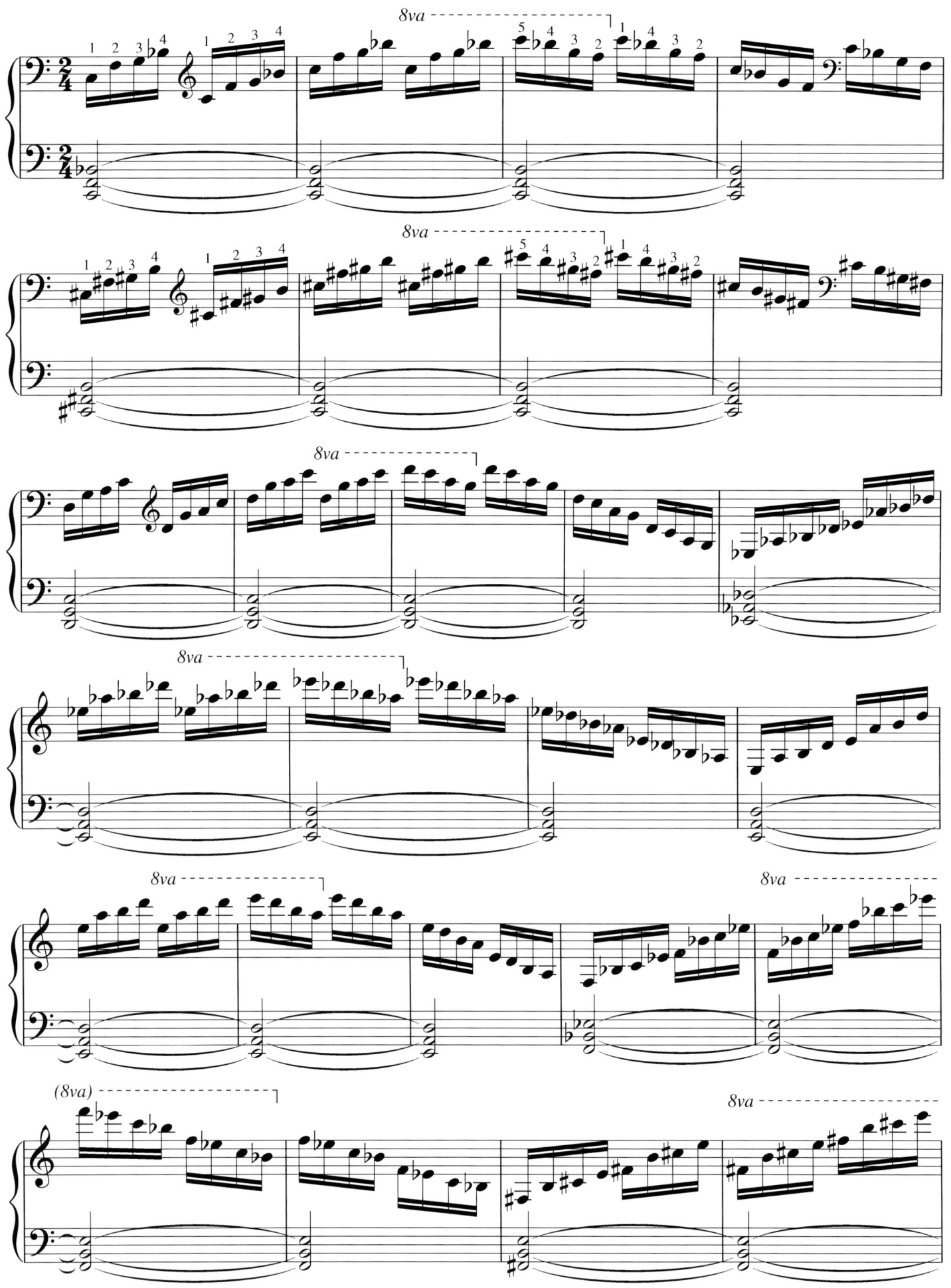

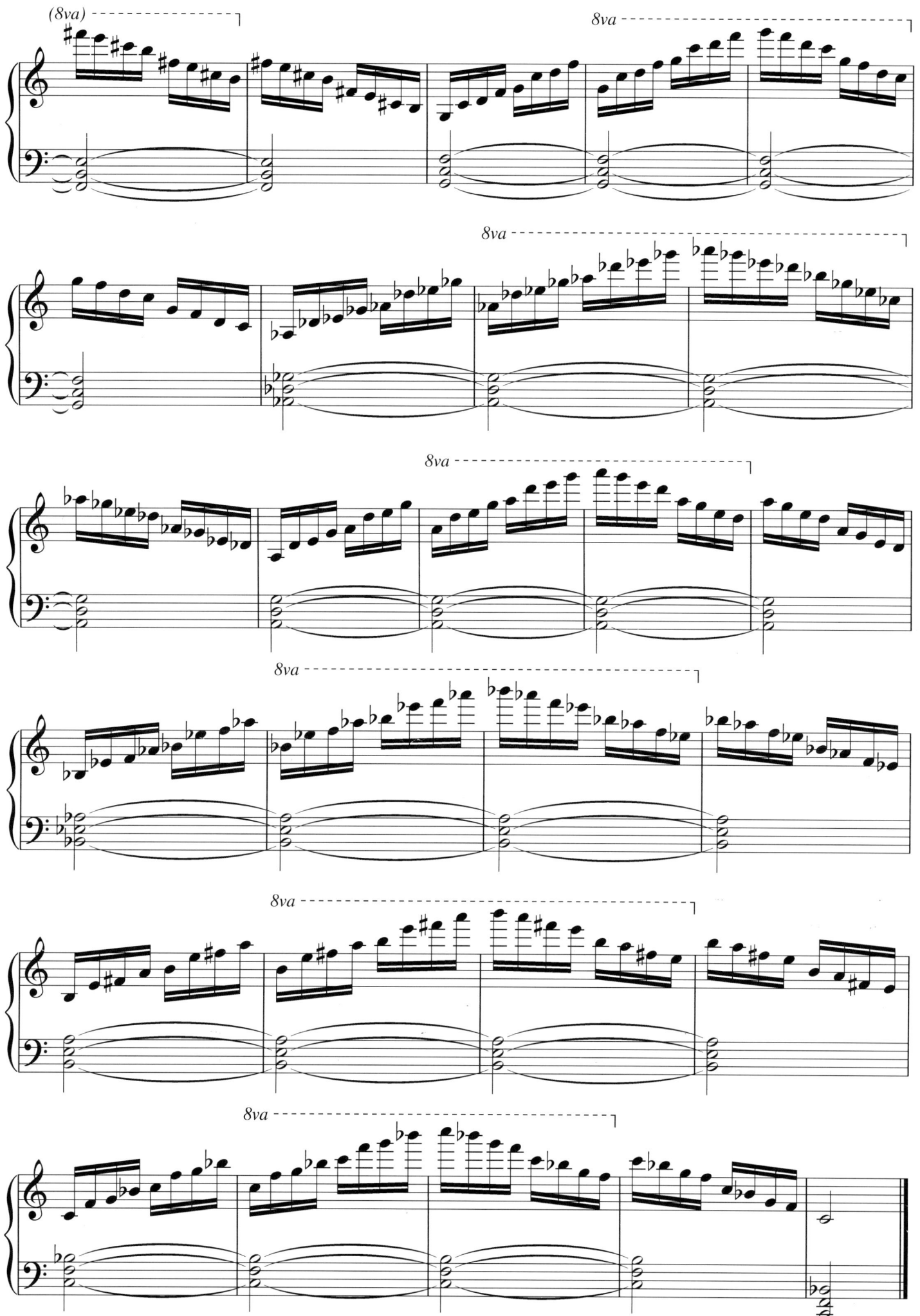

50